LOVE & GRATITUDE

A CHILD'S MEMOIR
ROOTED IN YOU

Atosha Logan

LOVE & GRATITUDE

A CHILD'S MEMOIR
ROOTED IN YOU

Atosha Logan

COPYRIGHT © 2025 BY ATOSHA LOGAN

ALL RIGHTS RESERVED. NO PART OF THIS PUBLICATION MAY BE REPRODUCED, DISTRIBUTED, OR TRANSMITTED IN ANY FORM OR BY ANY MEANS, INCLUDING PHOTOCOPYING, RECORDING, OR OTHER ELECTRONIC OR MECHANICAL METHODS, OR OTHERWISE WITHOUT THE PRIOR WRITTEN PERMISSION OF THE AUTHOR, EXCEPT IN THE CASE OF BRIEF QUOTATIONS EMBODIED IN REVIEWS, ARTICLES, OR CRITICAL WORKS.

PLEASE NOTE THAT NO PART OF THIS BOOK MAY BE USED OR REPRODUCED IN ANY MANNER FOR THE PURPOSE OF TRAINING, ARTIFICIAL INTELLIGENCE TECHNOLOGIES, OR SYSTEMS.

FOR PERMISSION REQUESTS, CONTACT THE AUTHOR AT:
ATOSHA LOGAN, AUTHOR & PUBLISHER
INFO@ATOSHALOGAN.COM
WWW.ATOSHALOGAN.COM

ISBN: 978-1-7362267-4-2 (PAPERBACK) 978-1-7362267-5-9 (E-BOOK)
FIRST EDITION

PRINTED IN THE UNITED STATES OF AMERICA

COVER DESIGN: ATOSHA LOGAN
INTERIOR LAYOUT: ATOSHA LOGAN

About the Author

Atosha Logan is a woman of faith, strength, and purpose who has dedicated more than two decades to the field of education and is an author, life coach, and consultant. Guided by her unwavering belief in God, she has poured her heart into nurturing, mentoring, and leading others with integrity and personal motivation. Her journey reflects resilience, hope, and a deep commitment to uplifting and empowering others.

Beyond her professional calling, Atosha treasures the bonds of family and the importance of legacy. She believes that life's experiences are not only meant to be lived but also shared as testimonies of God's grace. Her passion for legacy and storytelling is rooted in a belief that God's grace carries us through every season. This memoir is her gift of love, hope, and inspiration for generations to come.

She continues to live out her purpose with faith at the center, striving to leave behind a legacy of inspiration, love, and unwavering trust in God.

Atosha Logan

info@atoshalogan.com
www.atoshalogan.com

ACKNOWLEDGEMENTS

This memoir is the reflection of many hearts and hands that have touched my life, and I am deeply grateful for each one.

God has BLESSED me with a wonderful husband and three children.

To my family—you are my foundation and my greatest source of love and support. Thank you for standing beside me through every season of joy and trial, and for reminding me daily of the meaning of unconditional love. I am grateful for the wisdom you've shared and the lessons that continue to guide my journey. Each of you has left an imprint on my story that cannot be erased.

To my close friends, thank you for your laughter, encouragement, and honesty. Your presence has been a light in both the brightest and darkest moments, and your belief in me gave me the courage to keep writing.

Most of all, I give thanks to God. Without His grace, strength, and faithfulness, none of this would have been possible. Every chapter of my life is a testament to His unfailing love.

The Legacy of Jerald & Willie Mae Williams shall continue through me!
A Legacy to Live For Inc.

ROOTED IN YOU

A Child's Memoir of Love & Gratitude

A Child's Memoir
Introduction

A CHILD'S STORY IS ONE OF WONDER, DISCOVERY, AND GROWTH. THIS MEMOIR INVITES READERS INTO THE WORLD OF INNOCENCE AND IMAGINATION, CAPTURING THE LAUGHTER, QUESTIONS, AND DREAMS THAT DEFINE CHILDHOOD. MORE THAN RECOLLECTIONS, THESE PAGES HOLD THE VOICE OF A CHILD'S HEART—HONEST, HOPEFUL, AND FULL OF LIGHT.

FROM THE ROOTS THAT ANCHOR US TO THE BRANCHES THAT STRETCH TOWARD NEW HORIZONS, THESE PAGES CAPTURE BOTH STRUGGLE AND VICTORY. EACH MEMORY SERVES AS A REMINDER THAT WHILE WE CANNOT CONTROL EVERY CIRCUMSTANCE, WE CAN SHAPE THE LEGACY WE LEAVE BEHIND.

THIS MEMOIR IS MORE THAN A STORY—IT'S AN INVITATION TO REFLECT ON YOUR OWN JOURNEY, TO HONOR THE MEMORIES THAT SHAPE YOU, AND TO BE INSPIRED TO LIVE WITH COURAGE AND HOPE. REMINDING YOU OF WHERE YOU'VE BEEN, WHO HAS WALKED BESIDE YOU, AND THE DREAMS STILL WAITING AHEAD.

OPEN THESE PAGES, TAKE PART IN THE JOURNEY, AND LET IT SPARK REFLECTION, CONVERSATION, AND CONNECTION IN YOUR OWN LIFE WITH GRACE, GRATITUDE, AND COURAGE.

A CHILD'S MEMOIR
Table of Content

ALL ABOUT ME (11)

FAMILY TREE (14)

MY FAMILY (17)

HOME & NEIGHBORHOOD (32)

SCHOOLING & LEARNING (46)

FRIENDS & PLAY (58)

TRADITIONS & HOLIDAYS (72)

FIRSTS & MILESTONES (84)

FEELINGS & BIG EMOTIONS (96)

ADVENTURES & TRAVEL (112)

HEROES & ROLE MODELS (124)

HOPES & DREAMS (137)

LIFE'S REFLECTIONS (152)

LETTER(S) TO LOVE ONE (153)

A CHILD'S MEMOIR OF LOVE & GRATITUDE

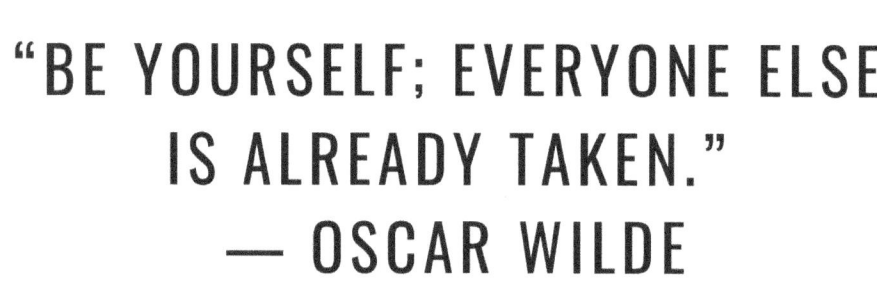

"BE YOURSELF; EVERYONE ELSE IS ALREADY TAKEN."
— OSCAR WILDE

A CHILD'S MEMOIR OF LOVE & GRATITUDE

All About ME

FULL NAME:

NICKNAME

DATE OF BIRTH

LOCATION

HOSPITAL

MOTHER

FATHER

FAVORITE COLOR(S)

PERSONALITY

WEIGHT AT BIRTH

HOME ADDRESS

PHONE NUMBER

SIBLINGS

FAVORITE MEAL

BREAKFAST

LUNCH

DINNER

SNACKS

RELIGION

FAVORITE BOOK(S)/SONG(S)

Capture the Moments

Add photos or draw pictures that represent this chapter of your life.

Memories

Memories

> "LIKE BRANCHES ON A TREE, WE ALL GROW IN DIFFERENT DIRECTIONS, YET OUR ROOTS REMAIN AS ONE."
> — ANONYMOUS

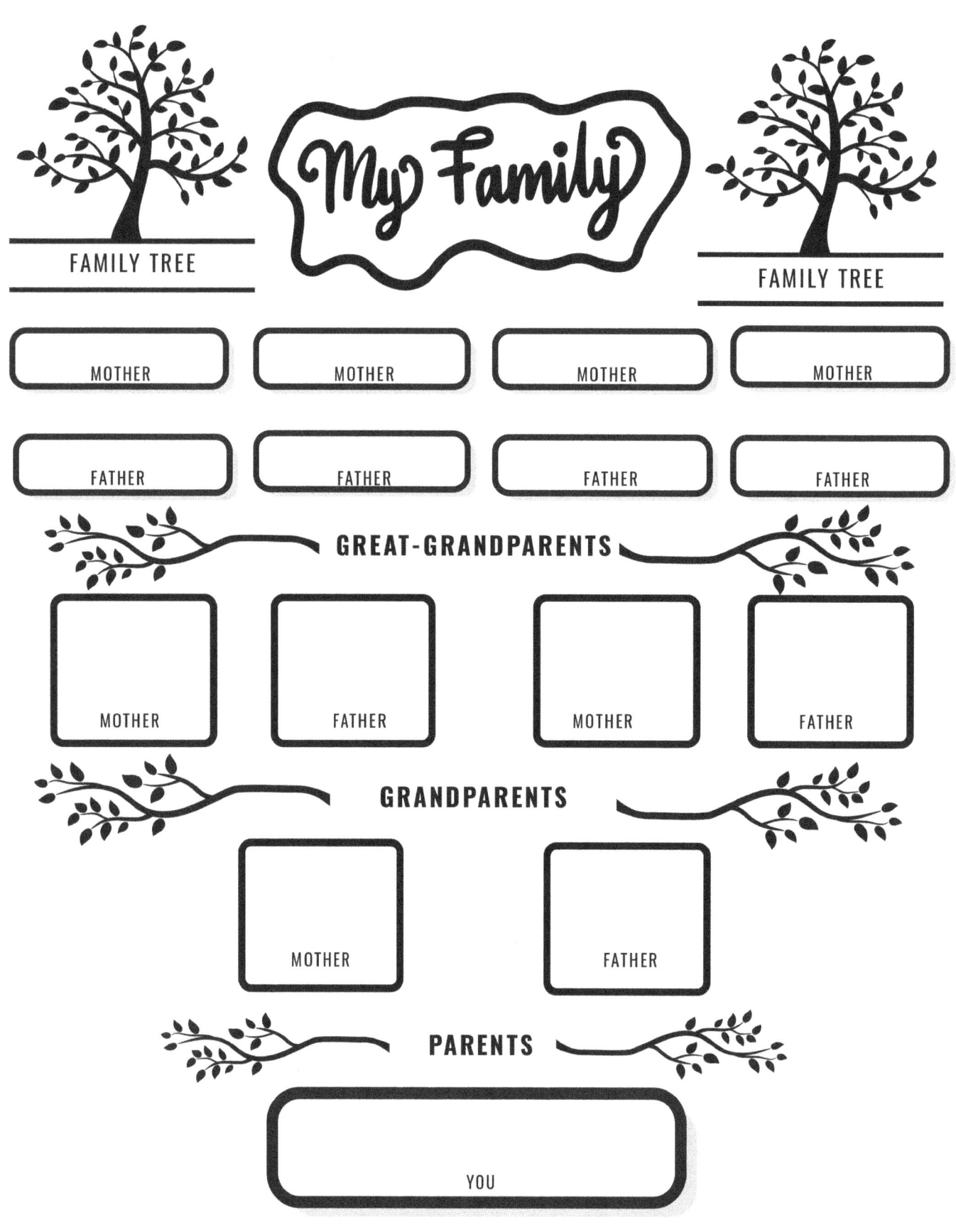

My Family

FAMILY TREE — FAMILY TREE

MOTHER — MOTHER — MOTHER — MOTHER

FATHER — FATHER — FATHER — FATHER

GREAT-GRANDPARENTS

MOTHER — FATHER — MOTHER — FATHER

GRANDPARENTS

MOTHER — FATHER

PARENTS

YOU

A CHILD'S MEMOIR OF LOVE & GRATITUDE

Capture the Moments

Add photos or draw pictures that represent this chapter of your life.

Memories

Memories

Memories

> "THE STORIES WE LIVE BECOME THE STORIES WE LEAVE BEHIND."
> — ANONYMOUS

ROOTED IN YOU

MY FAMILY

A CHILD'S MEMOIR OF
LOVE & GRATITUDE

WHO IS IN YOUR FAMILY?

WHAT MAKES EACH PERSON SPECIAL TO YOU?

WHAT IS A FAVORITE MEMORY YOU HAVE WITH YOUR FAMILY?

DESCRIBE A FAMILY RULE THAT HELPS YOUR HOME RUN SMOOTHLY.

_____
_____
_____
_____
_____
_____
_____
_____

WHAT IS SOMETHING YOUR FAMILY ALWAYS SAYS OR JOKES ABOUT?

_____
_____
_____
_____
_____
_____
_____
_____

HOW DOES YOUR FAMILY CELEBRATE BIG MOMENTS?

WHAT IS A MEAL YOUR FAMILY MAKES THAT YOU LOVE?

WHAT IS A STORY YOUR FAMILY TELLS AGAIN AND AGAIN?

WHAT IS YOUR FAVORITE PLACE TO BE TOGETHER AS A FAMILY?

WHO ARE YOUR CHOSEN FAMILY?

HOW DID THOSE BONDS FORM?

WHAT IS A TIME YOUR FAMILY HELPED YOU WHEN YOU NEEDED IT?

additional notes

additional notes

Capture The Moments

Add photos or draw pictures that represent this chapter of your life.

Memories

Memories

> "WE DO NOT REMEMBER DAYS, WE REMEMBER MOMENTS."
> — CESARE PAVESE

ROOTED IN YOU

HOME & NEIGHBORHOOD

A CHILD'S MEMOIR OF LOVE & GRATITUDE

WHAT DOES YOUR ROOM LOOK LIKE?

WHAT DO YOU LOVE ABOUT IT?

DESCRIBE YOUR NEIGHBORHOOD.

WHAT DO YOU SEE, HEAR, AND SMELL OUTSIDE?

WHO ARE YOUR NEIGHBORS, AND HOW DO YOU KNOW THEM?

WHAT DOES YOUR IDEAL HOME FEEL LIKE?

WHAT VALUES DOES IT EXPRESS?

WHAT CHORES DO YOU DO AT HOME?

HOW DO THEY HELP YOUR FAMILY?

WHAT DO YOU NOTICE WHEN THE SEASONS CHANGE WHERE YOU LIVE?

WHAT IS SOMETHING YOU WOULD CHANGE ABOUT YOUR HOME IF YOU COULD?

WRITE ABOUT A JOURNEY THAT CHANGED YOUR SENSE OF HOME.

HOW HAS MOVING (OR STAYING PUT) FORMED YOU?

WHAT IS A SOUND YOU HEAR AT HOME THAT MAKES YOU FEEL SAFE?

WHAT IS A SPECIAL PLACE IN YOUR HOUSE AND WHY?

additional notes

additional notes

Capture the Moments

Add photos or draw pictures that represent this chapter of your life.

Memories

Memories

Memories

> "OUR MOST TREASURED FAMILY HEIRLOOMS ARE OUR SWEET FAMILY MEMORIES."
> — ANON

ROOTED IN YOU

SCHOOL & LEARNING

A CHILD'S MEMOIR OF LOVE & GRATITUDE

WHAT IS YOUR FAVORITE SUBJECT AT SCHOOL?

WHY?

WHO IS A TEACHER WHO MAKES LEARNING FUN FOR YOU?

DESCRIBE A PROJECT YOU WORKED HARD ON AND FELT PROUD OF.

WHAT IS A TIME YOU TRIED SOMETHING NEW AT SCHOOL?

_____
_____
_____
_____
_____
_____
_____
_____

WHAT HELPS YOU FEEL BRAVE WHEN YOU ANSWER A QUESTION IN CLASS?

_____
_____
_____
_____
_____
_____
_____
_____
_____

WHAT IS A BOOK YOU ENJOYED?

WHAT DID YOU LIKE ABOUT IT?

WHAT IS A GOAL YOU HAVE FOR SCHOOL?

HOW WILL YOU REACH IT?

WHAT IS SOMETHING YOU CAN TEACH SOMEONE ELSE TO DO?

additional notes

additional notes

Capture the Moments

Add photos or draw pictures that represent this chapter of your life.

Memories

Memories

> "IN EVERY CONCEIVABLE MANNER, THE FAMILY IS THE LINK TO OUR PAST, BRIDGE TO OUR FUTURE."
> — ALEX HALEY

ROOTED IN YOU

FRIENDS & PLAY

A CHILD'S MEMOIR OF
LOVE & GRATITUDE

WHO IS YOUR BEST FRIEND?

WHAT MAKES YOUR FRIENDSHIP SPECIAL?

WHAT IS A PLACE WHERE YOU AND YOUR FRIENDS LIKE TO GO TOGETHER?

WHAT ACTIVITY MAKES YOU LOSE TRACK OF TIME?

DESCRIBE A COLLECTION, HOBBY, OR CRAFT THAT BRINGS YOU JOY.

WHAT GAMES DO YOU LOVE TO PLAY, INSIDE OR OUTSIDE?

DESCRIBE A TIME YOU SHARED OR TOOK TURNS KINDLY.

WHAT IS A TIME YOU SOLVED A PROBLEM WITH A FRIEND?

WHAT DO YOU LIKE TO DO WHEN YOU HAVE FREE TIME?

WHAT MAKES YOU LAUGH SO HARD YOU CAN'T STOP?

WHAT ARE YOUR FAVORITE TOYS OR ACTIVITIES RIGHT NOW?

WHAT IS A NEW FRIEND YOU MADE RECENTLY AND HOW DID YOU MEET?

WHAT'S A TEAM OR CLUB YOU ENJOY?

WHAT'S FUN ABOUT IT?

additional notes

additional notes

Capture the Moments

Add photos or draw pictures that represent this chapter of your life.

Memories

Memories

Memories

> "WE ARE SHAPED AND FASHIONED BY WHAT WE LOVE."
> — JOHANN WOLFGANG VON GOETHE

ROOTED IN YOU

TRADITIONS & HOLIDAYS

A CHILD'S MEMOIR OF
LOVE & GRATITUDE

WHAT IS YOUR FAVORITE HOLIDAY?

HOW DO YOU CELEBRATE IT?

WHAT SPECIAL FOODS DO YOU EAT ON HOLIDAYS OR BIRTHDAYS?

_____
_____
_____
_____
_____
_____
_____
_____
_____
_____

WHAT DECORATIONS MAKE YOUR HOME FEEL FESTIVE?

_____
_____
_____
_____
_____
_____
_____
_____
_____
_____

WHAT SONGS OR MUSIC DO YOU HEAR DURING SPECIAL TIMES?

WHAT IS A TRADITION YOUR FAMILY HAS THAT YOU LOVE?

DESCRIBE A BIRTHDAY YOU REMEMBER WELL.

WHAT IS A NEW TRADITION YOU WOULD LIKE TO START?

WHAT IS A GIFT YOU GAVE SOMEONE THAT MADE THEM SMILE?

WHAT IS A PLACE YOU LIKE TO VISIT DURING HOLIDAYS?

WHAT IS A FAMILY STORY YOU HEAR DURING CELEBRATIONS?

additional notes

additional notes

Capture the Moments

Add photos or draw pictures that represent this chapter of your life.

Memories

Memories

> "IT IS NOT LENGTH OF LIFE, BUT DEPTH OF LIFE."
> — RALPH WALDO EMERSON

A CHILD'S MEMOIR OF LOVE & GRATITUDE

ROOTED IN YOU

FIRSTS & MILESTONES

A CHILD'S MEMOIR OF LOVE & GRATITUDE

WHAT IS SOMETHING YOU LEARNED TO DO THIS YEAR FOR THE FIRST TIME?

WRITE ABOUT YOUR FIRST DAY AT A NEW SCHOOL OR CLASS.

WHAT WAS IT LIKE TO LOSE YOUR FIRST TOOTH (OR LEARN TO RIDE A BIKE, ETC.)?

_____
_____
_____
_____
_____
_____
_____
_____

WHAT IS THE FIRST BIG TRIP YOU REMEMBER TAKING?

_____
_____
_____
_____
_____
_____
_____
_____
_____

WHAT IS A CERTIFICATE, RIBBON, OR AWARD YOU EARNED—WHAT DID IT MEAN TO YOU?

WHO HELPED YOU WHEN YOU TRIED SOMETHING NEW?

WHAT IS A TIME YOU FELT VERY PROUD OF YOURSELF?

WHAT IS SOMETHING YOU USED TO FIND HARD THAT IS EASIER NOW?

WHAT IS A GOAL YOU REACHED—HOW DID YOU DO IT?

DESCRIBE A NEW RESPONSIBILITY YOU HAVE AT HOME OR SCHOOL.

additional notes

additional notes

Capture the Moments

Add photos or draw pictures that represent this chapter of your life.

Memories

Memories

> "LIFE CAN ONLY BE UNDERSTOOD BACKWARDS; BUT IT MUST BE LIVED FORWARDS."
> — SØREN KIERKEGAARD

ROOTED IN YOU

FEELINGS & BIG EMOTIONS

A CHILD'S MEMOIR OF LOVE & GRATITUDE

WHAT HELPS YOU WHEN YOU FEEL WORRIED OR SCARED?

WHO DO YOU TALK TO WHEN YOU'RE SAD?

WHAT IS A TIME YOU FELT VERY HAPPY —WHAT HAPPENED?

WHAT IS A TIME YOU FELT FRUSTRATED?

HOW DID YOU CALM DOWN?

HOW DO YOU PROCESS LOSS OR DISAPPOINTMENT?

WHAT IS A PLACE THAT HELPS YOU FEEL PEACEFUL?

WHAT DOES KINDNESS LOOK LIKE TO YOU?

WHEN DID YOU CHOOSE COURAGE OVER COMFORT?

WHAT BOUNDARY DID YOU SET THAT PROTECTED YOUR WELL-BEING?

HOW DID YOU REBUILD TRUST AFTER IT WAS BROKEN?

WHEN DO YOU FEEL MOST CONFIDENT AND WHY?

HOW DO YOU SHOW LOVE TO PEOPLE YOU CARE ABOUT?

WHAT IS A TIME YOU APOLOGIZED AND MADE THINGS RIGHT?

WHEN DO YOU FEEL BRAVE?

WHAT HELPS YOU BE BRAVE?

additional notes

additional notes

Capture the Moments

Add photos or draw pictures that represent this chapter of your life.

Memories

Memories

> "THE MEANING OF LIFE IS TO FIND YOUR GIFT. THE PURPOSE OF LIFE IS TO GIVE IT AWAY."
> — PABLO PICASSO

ROOTED IN YOU

ADVENTURES & TRAVEL

A CHILD'S MEMOIR OF
LOVE & GRATITUDE

WHERE HAVE YOU GONE ON A TRIP THAT YOU REMEMBER WELL?

WHAT DID YOU PACK FOR A SPECIAL ADVENTURE?

WHAT IS A NEW FOOD YOU TRIED SOMEWHERE NEW?

WHAT ANIMAL OR PLANT DID YOU SEE THAT AMAZED YOU?

WHAT IS AN OUTDOOR PLACE YOU LOVE— WHAT DO YOU DO THERE?

WHAT IS A TIME YOU EXPLORED A MUSEUM, PARK, OR TRAIL?

WHO DO YOU LIKE TO TRAVEL WITH AND WHY?

WHAT IS A LANDMARK OR BUILDING YOU THOUGHT WAS COOL?

WHAT IS A FUNNY TRAVEL STORY YOU LIKE TO TELL?

WHAT DREAM TRIP OR EXPERIENCE IS STILL ON YOUR LIST—WHY?

additional notes

additional notes

Capture The Moments

Add photos or draw pictures that represent this chapter of your life.

Memories

Memories

> "THE GREATEST USE OF LIFE IS TO SPEND IT FOR SOMETHING THAT WILL OUTLAST IT."
> — WILLIAM JAMES

ROOTED IN YOU

HEROES & ROLE MODELS

A CHILD'S MEMOIR OF
LOVE & GRATITUDE

WHO DO YOU LOOK UP TO AT HOME, SCHOOL, OR IN YOUR COMMUNITY?

WHAT MAKES SOMEONE A HERO IN YOUR EYES?

WHO ENCOURAGES YOU TO BE YOUR BEST SELF?

WHAT IS A TIME SOMEONE STOOD UP FOR YOU OR HELPED YOU?

WHO DO YOU WANT TO THANK FOR BELIEVING IN YOU?

WHAT IS A CHARACTER FROM A BOOK OR SHOW YOU ADMIRE—WHY?

WHAT IS A TALENT OR SKILL YOU WANT TO LEARN FROM SOMEONE?

WHO MAKES YOUR WORLD FEEL SAFER AND KINDER?

WHAT IS A KINDNESS YOU SAW SOMEONE DO THAT YOU WON'T FORGET?

HOW DO YOU TRY TO BE A ROLE MODEL FOR YOUNGER KIDS?

additional notes

additional notes

Capture the Moments

Add photos or draw pictures that represent this chapter of your life.

Memories

Memories

Memories

> "THE GREATEST THING YOU'LL EVER LEARN IS JUST TO LOVE AND BE LOVED IN RETURN."
> — EDEN AHBEZ

A CHILD'S MEMOIR OF LOVE & GRATITUDE

ROOTED IN YOU

HOPES & DREAMS

A CHILD'S MEMOIR OF LOVE & GRATITUDE

WHAT DO YOU WANT TO BE REMEMBERED FOR?

BY WHOM?

WHAT STORIES DO YOU HOPE FUTURE GENERATIONS WILL TELL ABOUT YOU?

IF YOUR LIFE HAD A MOTTO, WHAT WOULD IT BE?

_____
_____
_____
_____
_____
_____
_____
_____

WHAT IS SOMETHING YOU WANT TO TRY BUT HAVEN'T YET?

_____
_____
_____
_____
_____
_____
_____
_____

WHAT KIND OF PERSON DO YOU WANT TO BE AS YOU GROW UP?

WHAT IS A BIG WISH YOU HAVE FOR YOUR FAMILY?

WHAT ARE THREE GOALS YOU HAVE FOR THE NEXT YEAR?

WHAT DO YOU HOPE THE NEXT CHAPTER OF YOUR LIFE HOLDS?

WHAT INVENTION WOULD YOU LIKE TO CREATE TO HELP OTHERS?

WHAT JOB OR HOBBY SOUNDS FUN TO YOU IN THE FUTURE?

WHAT IS A MESSAGE YOU WOULD LIKE TO GIVE YOUR FUTURE SELF?

additional notes

additional notes

Capture the Moments

Add photos or draw pictures that represent this chapter of your life.

Memories

Memories

Memories

> "OWNING OUR STORY AND LOVING OURSELVES THROUGH THAT PROCESS IS THE BRAVEST THING WE'LL EVER DO."
> — BRENÉ BROWN

Life's *Reflections*

(Overview)
SUMMARIZE KEY EVENTS

(Achievements)
WHAT WERE YOUR MAJOR ACHIEVEMENTS?

(Gratitude)
LIST THREE THINGS YOU'RE MOST GRATEFUL FOR.

(Priorities)
IDENTIFY KEY PRIORITIES AND GOALS.

○ _____
○ _____
○ _____
○ _____
○ _____

Dear _____,
LETTER TO LOVED ONE

_____
_____
_____
_____
_____
_____
_____
_____
_____
_____
_____
_____
_____
_____
_____
_____
_____
_____
_____

WITH LOVE,

_____

Dear _____,

LETTER TO LOVED ONE

WITH LOVE,

_____

Dear _____,

Letter to Loved One

_____
_____
_____
_____
_____
_____
_____
_____
_____
_____
_____
_____
_____
_____
_____
_____
_____
_____
_____
_____

WITH LOVE,

_____

Dear LETTER TO LOVED ONE

_____,

WITH LOVE,

_____

Dear _____,

LETTER TO LOVED ONE

WITH LOVE,

_____

Capture the Moments

Add photos or draw pictures that represent this chapter of your life.

Memories

Memories

Capture the Moments
Add photos or draw pictures that represent this chapter of your life.

Memories

Memories

"YOUR STORY IS WHAT YOU HAVE, WHAT YOU WILL ALWAYS HAVE. IT IS SOMETHING TO OWN."
— MICHELLE OBAMA

A CHILD'S MEMOIR OF LOVE & GRATITUDE

ADDITIONAL MEMOIR PUBLICATIONS

THE LIGHT THAT LINGERS
A PERSONAL MEMOIR OF LOVE AND LIFE

CARRIED IN MY HEART
A MOTHER'S MEMOIR OF LOVE AND LEGACY

GUIDED BY MY HANDS
A FATHER'S MEMOIR OF LOVE AND STRENGTH

BOUND BY OUR VOWS
A SPOUSE'S MEMOIR OF LOVE AND DEVOTION

FOR MORE INFORMATION OR
TO PURCHASE ADDITIONAL COPIES
WWW.ATOSHALOGAN.COM

Every life tells a story...

A child's story is one of wonder, discovery, and growth. This memoir invites readers into the world of innocence and imagination, capturing the laughter, questions, and dreams that define childhood. More than recollections, these pages hold the voice of a child's heart—honest, hopeful, and full of light.

More than a record of one life, this memoir is an invitation to reflect on your own story. It is a reminder that while we cannot choose every circumstance, we can choose the legacy we leave behind.

Whether you are seeking encouragement, reflection, or simply a heartfelt story, this book offers something to carry with you. May it inspire you to embrace your own journey with gratitude, courage, and love.

Atosha Logan is a woman of faith, strength, and purpose who has dedicated more than two decades to the field of education and is an author, certified life coach, consultant, Founder and CEO of A Legacy To Live For Inc. Guided by her unwavering belief in God, she has poured her heart into nurturing, mentoring, and leading others with integrity and personal motivation. Her journey reflects resilience, hope, and a deep commitment to uplifting and empowering others.

www.ingramcontent.com/pod-product-compliance
Lightning Source LLC
Chambersburg PA
CBHW081359070526
44583CB00020B/2594